I0049120

REAL ESTATE INVESTING

A Guide for Real Estate Agents and Investors

(Effective Strategies for Growing Your Real Estate Business Online)

Gilbert Crouch

Published by Bella Frost

Gilbert Crouch

All Rights Reserved

All Rights Reserved

Real Estate Investing: A Guide for Real Estate Agents and Investors (Effective Strategies for Growing Your Real Estate Business Online)

ISBN 978-1-77485-286-6

All rights reserved. No part of this guide may be reproduced in any form without permission in writing from the publisher except in the case of brief quotations embodied in critical articles or reviews.

Legal & Disclaimer

The information contained in this book is not designed to replace or take the place of any form of medicine or professional medical advice. The information in this book has been provided for educational and entertainment purposes only.

The information contained in this book has been compiled from sources deemed reliable, and it is accurate to the best of the Author's knowledge; however, the Author cannot guarantee its accuracy and validity and cannot be held liable for any errors or omissions. Changes are periodically made to this book. You must consult your doctor or get professional medical advice before using any of the suggested remedies, techniques, or information in this book.

Upon using the information contained in this book, you agree to hold harmless the Author from and against any damages, costs, and expenses, including any legal fees potentially resulting from the application of any of the information provided by this guide. This disclaimer applies to any damages or injury caused by the use and application, whether directly or indirectly, of any advice or information presented, whether for breach of contract, tort, negligence, personal injury, criminal intent, or under any other cause of action.

You agree to accept all risks of using the information presented inside this book. You need to consult a professional medical practitioner in order to ensure you are both able and healthy enough to participate in this program.

Table of Contents

Introduction

I would like to welcome all of you who are here for a visit to Think about and grow Wealth. My aim is to assist you in understanding the ways to succeed in real estate. My aim is to help you in the right direction and help you change your perspective ensure that you realize that money is a powerful instrument to create wealth by using the money of others and become the person you've always desired to be. When you invest in real property, you're helping others as well as the community, and you're creating money, and that's exactly what is the purpose of our existence right?

Chapter 1: What is A Property Survey?

Encumbrances and easements should be recorded on the title to the property and must be made public by the seller to ensure you are aware of the restrictions put on the deed of the property. Sometimes, it's helpful to conduct a survey on the property you intend to buy or sell to have a clear legally-enforceable description of boundaries for your home, and to be aware of any easements or encroachments. Surveys are professional, on-site measurement of property's lot lines and the dimensions of a house and the position of any improvement (such as the construction of a house) on the property as well as any encroachments which may exist, as well as easements (gas electric, gas, etc.) that are public records.

It is important to note that a spot survey may include additional measurements for any improvements. Surveyors employ a datum as a reference point to measure elevation. Developers are required to submit a site plan which incorporates information from a survey but includes the additional construction, such as roads being constructed and other improvements that the developer plans to build. Site plans that include survey information and plat maps are filed in offices of the county. They are available to you however you can request an updated survey done. There are three types of surveys used to establish the boundaries of the property.

Bounds and Metes The Metes are compass-based leading and direction (0-90 degrees) and bounds are the physical fixtures that serve as point of reference. For instance the property that is located at the address "9320 Duck Harbor Road, Plymouth, Michigan 48170' was registered in the property tax offices of the county in the form the following:

COM AT E 1/4 POST OF SEC, TH S 1 DEG 05' E 112.42 FT IN E LINE OF SEC, TH S 66 DEG 08' W 702.70 FT IN CENT OF HWY FOR PL OF BEG, TH S 14 DEG 06' E 850.03 FT, TH S 66 DEG 09' W 244.27 FT, TH N 22 DEG 40' W 542.46 FT, TH N 66 DEG 09' E 843.26 FT IN CENT OF HWY TO THE PL OF BEG, SEC 2, T2S-R7E, 3.62 AC

Block and Lot: These are plat reference numbers, or maps showing the property's divisions. A rectangular system of government is divided up the country into six-mile squares that are further subdivided. Every 36-square mile township can be divided in one sq mile segments (640 acres) which are then subdivided into quarter sections, and then into quarter sections and so on. This system of surveying is not usually used on the east coast. It is often referred to in the Public Land Survey System (PLSS). Every survey system requires reference lines or points. The more precise distance descriptions are linked to both the vertical (north towards south) principal Meridian line, as well as the horizontal (east to west) baseline. It has 37 main Meridian lines. The main Meridian line is a parallel vertical line six miles apart, referred to range lines. The township line is a parallel horizontal lines that are 6 miles apart. These lines are referred to as township lines.

A property that is located in the top portion of the northeast section 4 of Somerville Township would be recorded (and read from left to right) as N 1/2 Section 4 Township Somerville.

TRANSFER OF TITLE & DEEDS

Many new homeowners make the mistake of confusing the terms deed and ownership of the land. They are two distinct legal notions. Title is a legal right and deeds are legally binding document which grants the right. In accordance with the Statute of Frauds, a deed must be signed (and certified) document in order to be valid. If your property is in good and undisputed, then you are the owner of both the title and deed to the land. This distinction is because you are able to have title to the property, but you will not own the deed since somebody else has the property but doesn't make use of it as a lender, as an example.

A deed is a legal document in Latin or, as it is related to property, it is a legal transaction. A deed is known as an instrument to convey and the prior owner (grantor) transfers their property (grantee). It includes the party (principal) information as well as property information, a grant clause or 'hereby conveys' ...' as well as a havedum clause, which transfers all rights of the property.

A Grantor is known as a 'party of one part', and the grantee as 'party to that second component'. Only the Grantor has to sign the deed unless restrictions on property are being transferred like a mortgage , or obligations for a condominium unit, where the grantee is also required to acknowledge the title.

The deed has to be acknowledged or witnessed by an official witness, usually by a notary, to show that it's voluntary (i.e. mafia bosses cannot oblige you to acknowledge that deed, but they can oblige the notary to sign the deed).

The deed is referred to as an deed-poll and can't be accepted until handed over to the grantor. Once the deed has been acknowledged, it is recorded in the office of the county clerk in the county in which the property is located.

The deed should contain legal descriptions of the property to ensure you are not in any doubt over who is the owner. The language could be confusing to someone who is reading this for the very first time. For a refresher that the various methods of describing properties are like this:

Metes (angle and distance) and bounds (landmarks).

Reference, plat, or lot and Block: Using existing tax maps or other instruments to identify the property.

Monument: surveyors are able to place iron rods into the ground to indicate boundaries of the property. Iron rods are referred to as monuments despite the fact that the original description of the property was based on actual monuments that wouldn't ever be taken off the property. This is a dated system.

Rectangular survey system used since 1785 and referred to as the federal land survey system. It divides the nation in townships (36 sq miles) with each square mile further divided into sections (1 square mile equals the equivalent of 640 acres) and then to quarter section or quarter quarter (one eighth) sections.

Types of DEEDS

The deed that you sign is accompanied by certain rights. Depending on the rights transferred, you could be issued different types of deeds. A complete covenant or general deed includes the common 6 types of covenants, which include:

Contract of Seisin: It is the grantor who in fact has the title.

Contract of the right to transfer The grantor has the capacity and right to transfer the title.

Covenant against encumbrances: A promise that there aren't any unreported titles that are encumbered.

Covenant of tranquil enjoyment: a promise that the grantee is able to enjoy their new home without interruption due to an unidentified title defect. Title defect is greater than an encumbrance that could include in the form of physical (easement) or money (lien). A title defect occurs when other people can claim title or ownership of the property because of an encumbrance, or due to a legal claim on the property.

Covenant for additional assurances: a promises to repair any defects in the title and to make an efforts for any other assurances that the grantee might require.

Warranty: The grantor is responsible for defending and warranting the title against all individuals who claim ownership (should they turn up after having signed the deed).

The Bargain and Sale Deed doesn't include all the six common covenants and does not contain the most crucial warranty covenant. A bargain and sale deed that includes the warranty covenant is called a special warranty deed. These properties are offered at a discounted price because of this, and there are investors who are willing to take on the risk that they do not have all 6 covenants to ensure the lowest price. The company selling these properties doesn't want to invest time and money figuring out the legality and scope of different covenants and sells the property 'as is'.

Real Estate Owned (REO) or tax-lien property typically have sold and bargain deeds. Other circumstances that can create bargain and Sale deeds include the Executor's and Referee's deeds.

Executor or court-ordered deeds are bargains and sale deeds which allow those with special authority, such as the courts or executor of the estate owned by a dead individual to transfer title and deed to a property to somebody who is not the owner, generally without warranty.

Referee deeds are utilized to convey a title containing the agreement that a property is owned or Seisin during an auction for bankruptcy or foreclosure to the most bidder. Other covenants aren't generally secured (again as it is inefficient to the lender or another lender who is trying to dispose of those properties).

It is a Deed of Trust is a trust, which means it has three parties: the trustor, the beneficiary and the trustee. the trustee is able to hold this deed till the trustee is able to fulfill their obligations, such as repaying the loan. At that point, the deed transfers from the trustor to the beneficiary.

Quitclaim deeds are a straightforward contract that prohibits the grantor from claiming to this property at a later date. It does not contain any other covenants other than the seisin covenant. Let's take an example: your husband died and left the home he had rented out, which you purchased together when married to his lovely office assistant. You could be so upset that you'd never be able to contest your transfer at the time, but the lawyer for the young lady would require you to make a quitclaim declaration while you're still in a state of discontent to stop the possibility of ever trying to claim the title in the future.

Chapter 2: Knowing Your Market

It's not enough just to look at the house for sale at a fair price and to purchase it. You must know the type of market you're investing your money in. What that means is knowing the type of home values that are being realized in the area, and what they have to offer since those houses are likely to be your primary competition. One of the biggest errors you could make is to purchase the house you want to buy expecting to market it on a market that's not feasible in the particular location. There are a variety of aspects to be aware of since the market is vast and can vary greatly.

The market for families

Family-friendly, the kind of location that's ideal is one that is family-friendly. It will be a place for recreation as well as a good garden, far from major roads, and it will be located within the same area as safe and adequate shopping areas and schools. Families are likely to have a lot of priorities. They require bedrooms that are enough to accommodate their entire family, however they might require a second bedroom. The most important thing for them is bathrooms with en-suites, though parents might enjoy the privilege to have an en-suite attached to their bedroom , to be away from the chaos of children and preferring separate bathrooms to be used by children. The home must be suitable for families. In particular the kitchen must be spacious and you should look at what's available locally. If all houses in the area have great kitchens, but the house you are considering doesn't have a great kitchen space, it may not be appealing enough to convince people to buy it. A family space is crucial and, if you have small children, you'll require a place where children can play while the parents are able to watch their children.

The market for families is dependent on the property being located situated in a location that is secure, so should you look at the type of house that you believe is suitable for families but isn't located in a safe zone, you're likely to attract people who are unable to afford living in a safe and family-friendly area and consequently it is less expensive than the price you can realize when weighing it against districts that provide the family with the amenities they want.

The bachelor pad

If you're looking at this market, the people in this group tend to be single and young and would like to be close to the places where they can be. Therefore, purchasing a tiny home in a suburban area that is not in the middle of the action isn't likely to be noticed in a positive manner. There is a chance that homes in a crowded town close to their workplace are more appealing for them due to the convenience of a quick journey to get there. The bachelor's apartment will offer a good entertainment area since young people require it. Compare similar homes in the same neighborhood. Some people might not require the biggest garden, but they might still require some outdoor space. They'll certainly need to park their vehicles and in the parking area of the property, parking is crucial.

The amount of bedrooms aren't essential in a bachelor's home but that they'll need friends to stay, which is why having a spare room will be crucial. It could also be necessary to have that essential walk-in closet and a very contemporary bathroom. These are things young and upcoming professionals will be seeking and a contemporary kitchen that has an island that fits their laid-back lifestyle to a T.

Business people

They're the professionals over 50 with no children. The ideal home for them will be a focal point. It should be located in a desirable area and have an executive interiors with all the modern conveniences people would want. They won't be concerned about being away from the bachelor pad because they're used to working by vehicle. They'll need parking space, an entertainment area , and most definitely an en-suite bathroom for every bedroom since they could be hosting business guests. The standard of a house for older business owners will need to be exceptional.

When you're researching your market, speak to real estate agents since they are familiar of the local market and can inform you about what is selling and where the market is struggling and the indicators you learn from them can be useful in determining whether you are able to succeed in selling your home within their specific area. If you're considering purchasing a property through a agents who sell homes, you should ask an agent who is a real estate professional about the market. The agent who is selling the property to you may have their own motives in trying to sell the house to you initially and could provide you with the information they believe you need to be hearing.

Chapter 3: The Reasons Why Landlords Select "Residential"?

Be aware that when it comes to real estate investing, a large portion of your work involves working with tenant. Commercial and residential tenants differ significantly. Let's look at the differences.

Residential:

The typical residential investment includes duplexes, houses apartment buildings, duplexes, etc. These rentals are primarily intended for personal use rather than renting them out for business purposes.

Residential rentals - Homes and duplexes typically have long time tenants that take greater care of and pride in the rental. Therefore, the ability to scale is more likely when compared to apartments.

Apartments are usually more affordable, while homes tend to be more attractive. Multi-family rental homes (apartments) are usually thought of as the easiest property to obtain tenants due to a variety of reasons. One of the most common reasons we're seeing nowadays is the downsizing of retirement. The norm is that families decision to move into a home so that they can spend their time with their children in a bigger space. But, when children are graduated and left and gone to college, there's no requirement for the extra bedrooms, and the upkeep required for the backyard as well as other facilities which aren't getting frequent usage. Many retirees "downsize" to apartments to live in a more relaxed environment with less chores to be able to handle, as well as more money from the sale the home. Although this is a well known and documented real estate phenomenon, it's the magnitude of the rate at which it's occurring that is quite extraordinary. In order to meet the growing demand could be extremely profitable for investors in apartments. It is something to think about. This is just one instance.

Multi-unit residential homes are much easier to find tenants because of the lower cost of rent that is a huge advantage. A multi-unit residential property allows you to spread out the cost. For instance, if you own a 10-unit residence and only one unit is rentable, then you're only missing around 10% of your total income. If, however, you own one-family house that is not rented out, then you're losing all of the revenue. My experience is that even though a single-family house has the potential to lose the loss of 100% of revenue and better tenants, homes attract more dependable tenants (if you manage it properly) and will stay for longer with rents that are higher. Additionally, they tend to maintain the property. The price of rental apartments tends to be lower, and consequently, you get the value you pay for. However, I have witnessed numerous commercial rental properties remain vacant for prolonged periods. It is best to lease to tenants you are certain will remain. Also, of note is that although commercial rental properties may be vacant for lengthy periods of time, the majority of commercial rentals are able to get long-term leases.

In some regions the residential properties are month-to-month. However, we're seeing that the majority of residential rental properties are being offered for leases of one year or more. This means that the chance of vacant spaces can be higher in an apartment, however the loss in rental revenue isn't as severe due to not impacting the whole structure.

The region can also be an important role. It's true that rental rates in most of California nowadays are quite expensive and tenants who rent are likely to pay more. The good thing is that the tenants typically tend to take better care of their property , which means you'll experience less hassles and costs later on. It might differ in different areas So, do your research regarding your particular area.

Commercial:

Commercial rentals include a variety of kinds of properties, including warehouses, offices and retail centers, building commercial land, etc.

When deciding on the best choice in commercial real estate take into consideration these aspects:

Commercial retail is a good option for tenants who are long-term. They typically

run their own business in these locations ,
and don't wish to deal with the stress of
moving their business and risk losing
customers. This is great news for you as it
means less time and effort to find new
tenants and generating rental revenue.

Warehouses for commercial use can enjoy
similar advantages when it's an
established company.

There is a higher risk of being a target for
an insurance claim in commercial rental
properties, especially those that are retail.
A higher volume of traffic flows in and out
of the property vs. homes that are rented
out to individuals or families.

You must be aware of the specifics of the
different types of commercial rental
properties and who and how they can be
rental. I have had experience working with
clients who are involved in:

1. A retail storefront that is commercial. It is likely that it is comparable to residential. A majority of these buildings are tiny and it is easier to maintain a tenant. Which retail establishment would relocate once they have an established address? There aren't many. The leases are usually extended for longer periods of duration.

2. Commercial warehouse rentals. They can be used for a company to run in , or as storage space for businesses (like construction companies). The advantages of these is that the maintenance may not be that great. There are a few amenities. The drawback is that it could take an extended period between tenants since the renters are specifically for this kind of structure (and perhaps the land). However, as with the retail space tenants managing these business are typically long-term tenants.

Chapter 4: Role of Private Credit Lines And Private Lending

Overview

Personal credit and "signature credits" can be obtained through the majority of credit unions or banks for those with a good credit score and regular income.

The Positive

Personal credit lines are an excellent source of money to pay for down payments or rehabilitation projects. They're typically "unsecured" meaning that they can ensure that your title home isn't impeded. The terms of loans can be secured for several years before the repayment deadline.

The Downside

Credit lines that are not secured can be restricted to $15,000-$20,000 or less. They typically have an interest rate of between 12% and 15% or more.

Success Strategy

The money can be utilized for long-term deals. For instance, if you purchase a property that is with financing already in place and require only minor repair (carpet or paint) it is a viable option to obtain the funds to make the repairs and let the rents be paid for a period of time.

Alternative Strategies

Strategy #8: Time For Hard Money

Overview

As a complement to the above methods as a backup to all the methods described above, hard money is a crucial component of your arsenal of funding especially when you begin to purchase multiple properties simultaneously. It is more costly than private funds, but is available in every city, for virtually every credit or project provided the numbers are sufficient.

The Positive

It is usually quick (3-10 days to pay) and doesn't require your credit score for approval. A majority of cash-back lenders have equity that means they lend on the value of the loan and not the lender.

The Downside

Charges for borrowing hard cash typically range from 3-5 points in on the front end, and then 11% to 15 percent interest. That's why I stated previously that borrowing hard money is costly. A lot of hard money lenders will only lend a portion of the purchase price that means you must get a second loan for the remaining portion of the purchase. Most lenders who offer hard money can only lend 12 or 6 months.

Success Strategy

If the moment should arrive when you've got an amazing deal that has a high profit margin, and you have there is no other method to fund your purchase, don't be afraid to contact a cash lender within your region. 5 points may seem expensive (okay it's costly!) However, compare that to the amount you'll earn upon the successful conclusion of the transaction. If you're making less than to justify the cost of 5 points, then the "deal" was not actually an "deal" at all. Be sure to have a plan for exit and a backup plan prior to purchasing a house using hard money. If you intend to flip the property, but it's not selling you must be in the process of negotiating less costly private money or a credit partner or wholesale buyers, to remove the lender with hard money before the balloon reaches maturity.

Strategy #9 9: Business Partnerships

Overview

Utilizing this method can be an effective option to begin from the beginning. You contribute effort and time, and you are the one who puts in the money and/or credit. You'll be able to split the gains from the transaction in advance.

The Positive

The deal is funded without using credit or cash You won't need to pay regular interest payments as the project is in progress.

The Downside

Offering 50% of the profit (or even more) of your deal can be a lot higher than paying couple of points and interest to a hard or private money lender.

Success Strategy

This is a great way to convince someone to help you start your business before you've established relationships with lenders who are confident in you. If you are having difficulty attracting lenders at the beginning of your venture You can make use of business partnerships to gain experience and establish a history to present private lenders that can assist you in gaining credibility and build confidence.

Chapter 5: Redesigning It

Once you've located and paid for the ugly duckling property then the real work begins when it's time to begin to do business and make it an evergreen swan that produces wealth. However, regardless of how skilled you might be, it's virtually impossible to go through all the steps by yourself . That's why the initial portion of this chapter contains the steps to form an effective team capable of supporting your efforts for the duration of your time operating in the real estate investing business. The only thing keeping everything from becoming a joke in forming an effective team is the cost associated with creating one. In reality, the phrase you pay for what you receive for is particularly relevant when it comes to hiring talented people. The most effective way to go is simply plan for the costs as you come up with your strategy to earn a profit from the asset.

If you are looking to create an efficient team that can help you achieve your real estate goals It is essential to begin with a lawyer well-versed in real estate as well as an accountant who is certified public that is specialized in the kind of investment you're entering into. While you should never be able to do much to accomplish for these professionals but if you come across a situation that you require their help, you'll be glad there are people on your payroll. These services are sure cost you money, but there isn't a standard cost for these costs, so it's not just be worth shopping around , but it's beneficial to bargain as well.

Find the best contractor

After you have got your legal counsel in place and you are ready to direct all your attention to choosing the most suitable general contractor is within your budget, and also as a backup option so that you know you'll never have to put off an overhaul after you've already made the decision to purchase the property. While an expert could be able tackle the level of renovation needed in a typical rental investment property, when you're taking a look at the ugly ducklings of real estate you'll find that in the majority of cases, there is too much to do to tackle everything on your own. This is why choosing the best general contractor crucial, as they'll be responsible for managing all the bigger tasks that need to be completed before the new investment can begin to earn money.

General contractors are the one who is entirely in charge of the construction schedule, and even having their own team on board so that you don't have to search for experts for every job. While finding the contractor who is the right fit for your needs may take time and costly, the benefits will be worth it many times over when you're finished investing in rental property. To aid you on your way, take a look at these suggestions.

Make suggestions For finding the most suitable general contractor for your needs the most efficient method to narrow your selection is to begin by obtaining the most recommendations you can get. If you're not yet involved with an investment group in your area, such as a local real estate group, you must begin, but for the time being you'll need to content your search on the website of the National Remodeling Institute to find members in your area who have been thoroughly scrutinized and verified. If your search yields nothing then the next location you can get some results is to ask an inspector in your area (who is also a person you should be sure to know) who they identify that can perform the best job. If you are looking for a contractor who is reliable and that stands out in the mind of someone who is looking at their work throughout the day is definitely an option. Similar to that, you could ask the proprietor of a local mill about the contractors who can be assured of purchasing the best quality materials.

Interviews for starters If you are not rushing into in-person interviews It is crucial to avoid wasting a lot of time and energy by speaking to people over the phone before you begin. You should inquire about the type of projects the contractor is responsible for as well as the quantity of jobs they handle at a time, details about the team, and references.

Face to face: Following the telephone interviews then the next step you'll want to arrange appointments for in-person interviews with the candidates you enjoyed the most. This is a crucial step that shouldn't be skipped since it allows you to talk about the particulars of your particular situation, while giving you a sense of the way you and the contractor work together. The contractor you select will be spending some time with you, so it is crucial to ensure that you are able to get along before you have already signed up to a contract.

Follow up: The final thing you'll need to do is be sure to follow-up in depth with the company you are thinking of using. It is crucial to be vigilant during this process because this is the person who you are relying on to make sure that your investment is legitimately turning to a profit. Doing not research their past and work history is like giving your investment capital to a conman on a silver platter , and that is why it is highly advised against.

Make a renovation on a dime

In the event of ensuring that your renovations will to go in the most efficient way however, at as little of a price as is anticipated, it is usually the key to success or failure for a lot of new real property investors. To ensure that things go according to plan, you should consider these tips to help reduce costs while keeping your tenants happy and satisfied.

Reduce every job down to the smallest of elements: contemplating everything that has to be accomplished to make your home ready for renters is often enough to induce you to start sweating, you will discover that the entire process is simpler to manage once you've broken down everything into its basic components. This will not only allow you to deal with the tasks that must be completed, but it will also aid in saving money since you'll be able identify all the necessary items in advance, which allows the possibility of obtaining a discounted price on large quantities. It is best to look through the rooms and create a list of all the tasks that must be accomplished so that you are able to review the list before listing the property to ensure you are able to ensure that all was completed according to the plan.

Consider where it's possible to save money: However, you'll need to take every step to remove any ugly duckling image that the property may have prior to attempting to let it out. It is important to take into consideration that renters aren't buyers, so you don't have to be concerned about making sure that everything is in order. As a guideline it is only going to need to make changes which you're sure will make the property more rented or boost the amount you will be able to charge when everything is done. The first thing you should do is will want to update the kitchen and bathrooms, which could be accomplished by swapping out the doors on cabinets as well as the fixtures and countertops. If you're looking to select the most affordable options, you could be able to remodel two rooms in a reasonable amount of about $1,000.

Always choose neutral colors: When you're changing your home's decor that has an impact on colors, you're likely to make sure to select neutral shades which can be easily incorporated into many colors, even though white isn't suggested. This will not only make it easier to meet the requirements of a range of renters, but it is also possible to locate neutral paint colors in the bargain box for just a few dollars of the cost it would originally. You may also be able to purchase the neutral colors of paint in bulk when they are in sale so that you are sure you will be able to paint between tenants for many long time to in the future.

Buy at a bargain, but don't purchase cheap Real estate investors looking to purchase rental properties for the first time are usually enticed to choose the cheapest items when it comes to satisfying a specific requirement. It's almost guaranteed to be a bad option, but they'll eventually discover that cheap items are worn out twice as fast than high-end ones, which means they will be more costly in the end. Be aware that products that are inexpensive are priced in accordance with their quality. It is best to take all costs in the air up in advance instead of waiting for the product that is cheap to require replacement more than once.

Establish relationships with suppliers: When it comes time to source materials for your renovations, it is essential to do the research in advance to ensure that you are able to get the best price you can get for the materials you are sure of purchasing in large quantities. In actuality, rushing to your local big-box store to purchase the last minute items is among the most unintentional sources of capital loss for new real estate investors because these small expenses aren't incorporated into the total expense of the project and therefore aren't accounted for until later on.

The convenience of purchasing your goods in bulk through a local retailer can not only enable you to calculate the price in advance and more precisely and also give you an opportunity to save money in addition. To experience these savings at work, all you'll need to do is look up the local hardware stores before speaking to an administrator.

When you've received the appropriate person's focus, all you have to do is share the list of items you need and explain to them that it is a long-term investment plan and that you're likely to purchase the items in bulk several times per year. If you have a clear understanding of what you're offering what you are offering, all you need to do is ask if there's something they can offer in exchange to ensure that you will purchase all of your essential items from their location. While this isn't going to work for all managers at each store but it will take only several attempts until you come across one who is willing to negotiate a deal.

Keep an eye on for new products: If you establish a routine of constantly looking for any products that might be helpful when renovating your home inexpensively, eventually you'll realize that you have more diverse set of options at hand in case you require them. If you are aware that a certain product is one you never seem to run out of at the most crucial moment, it might be worth the cost and effort to purchase it in bulk ahead of time and save yourself the stress later.

One area where is always worth being looking for the best price is when finding granite for smaller countertops. Nothing adds style to a room faster than granite countertops. However, the granite used for this effect is able to quickly become extremely expensive. Therefore it is important to are looking for granite with only significant flaws in one particular section, for instance, the area where the sink is in a countertop for bathrooms, then you could pick up huge chunks of granite for huge discounts.

Always make sure to do a cost/benefit analysis when you are deciding the kind of renovations you're likely to need to start with during the initial makeover of your ugly duckling it is essential that you consider the overall cost of the project into consideration not just in the immediate term, but over the long run too. Most of the time, you'll be offered options that might be suitable for the next group of renters, maybe one or two times, yet they will eventually require to be addressed in a permanent way. It is crucial to consider these options only with a focus on your budget, but also taking into consideration how much the cost of performing the same repair over and over again will be. If you can amortize the additional expenses of doing the work in the first place over a period of time, you will typically find that the expenses will be in balance or that the longer-lasting fix will end up being more affordable. A real estate rental property is a long-term investment, so make sure you consider it as such.

Chapter 6: How To Purchase Your First Property In Real Estate

You likely have taken time to research the local market and perhaps even contacted several sources for financing and have arranged for that too. After you've got everything done, it's time to begin taking the steps necessary to purchase your first house. There are specific steps to do to ensure you buy a property at an affordable price, and with minimal work needed on it, in order that you can get the job done while still making an excellent profit from the process. Once you've decided it's time to buy the initial investment home, be sure you go through the next steps:

The first step is to select the strategy you'd like to employ. This will aid in determining which properties you'd like to buy. Flipping and rental properties have different requirements.

It is also important to define the criteria you will use to select your property. What are you hoping to discover in your property? Do you want the property to be located in the same location? What's the budget you'd like to set? Are you planning to lease out the property to a family or just an individual? What amount of effort are you capable of putting into the property following the purchase? Knowing this information beforehand will enable you choose the best property without worrying about being distracted in your look.

Select the loan you'd like to utilize. Because most people aren't likely to have the entire amount of the property to purchase real estate, you'll usually have to depend on an institution like a bank or other for funding. You should take your time to look and before you submit an offer, you must be pre-approved for the loan you want to take out.

Explore online websites such as the MLS advertisements for yard signposts or even mailers to determine which homes are being offered for sale in your local area. You are able to do this by yourself, however certain people prefer working with a real estate agent to assist them in finding the home they are looking for. When you come across a property take the time to go through the criteria you specified in the first step to ensure that it is the best property to meet your requirements. It's always recommended to have a small amount of flexibility in the event of an opportunity that's great but falls a bit outside of your desired criteria, but stay as closely to your criteria as you can.

Offer to buy. You could collaborate with a realtor for this one. This is a good option for a first-time buyer purchasing your first house. The buyer will be the one to pay the agent, which means it won't cost you anything right now. Realtors are trained to manage the legalities of the selling process which is why they are an excellent resource. There are several methods you can employ when buying a house and they are based on the price the seller is willing to pay for the property as well as how much you can pay. Start with a bit of flexibility because the seller is to seek out a bargain about the price. Setting your price at your highest almost guarantees that you will get a loss.

Negotiate. The seller is likely to need to go exchanges with you to find the most competitive price possible. It is best to start with the price that's lower than what you're willing pay so that the seller is able to bargain with you. If the seller accepts your first offer, then you've made an extremely good deal. If they reject, you're in a position to make a second offer. If the seller accepts your offer and accepts it, the agent can help in writing your purchase contract. If you're working yourself and want to do it yourself, you can create the purchase agreement by yourself as well.

While you're waiting for the money to arrive and the seller has accepted the terms of your offer, be sure to complete all the necessary inspections. This will give you an idea of what issues exist that need to be addressed at the home. In the event of a problem and the terms of the contract that you have with your seller you may be able to convince the seller to take care of certain repairs, which can reduce time and cost. If you do not attend to these inspections, you'll be the one in charge of making sure that they are all repaired by yourself. Think about the possibility that the buyer who you are selling the home to will conduct inspections. By performing one today you will avoid problems during the next inspection.

At this point you must also begin speaking to contractors that can assist you in getting the job completed. Once the loan and financing go through and the timer starts to tick. The longer you are tied to the home, the more it will cost you to pay mortgage bills and more. Try to obtain estimates on what it will cost to carry out the work and then determine whether you are able to get the contractors in the house in the shortest amount of time after the closing. If you have a plan to carry the entire process out it is possible to finish the work in some weeks, meaning you could relist it or begin renting it out quickly.

After you've completed the inspections and are satisfied with the way they were conducted It is now time to visit the Title and Escrow office to complete all the documents required. After that, the paperwork will to be filed and you'll be legally the owner of the property. It is now time getting the house set up, have the contractors on board and begin to plan how you can earn money from the home. If you plan to let it out to tenants then you should begin listing the property for renters. If you are planning to sell the property, you must do the work quickly to be able to list the property and sell it. This must be completed as quickly as is possible.

The most important thing to keep in mind is that usually you get an occasional break before the first installment is due. It is usually approximately two months prior to the date you are required to make your first payment. Based on the agreement you have to the lender, you might be in a position to pay more in interest when closing, and also have the period of payment extended just slightly. Make use of this to complete the task quickly , without the need to pay for the house and perhaps you will save money along the way.

The procedure will be similar in the case of commercial or residential real estate, too. Always ensure that you're getting an excellent deal on the property you select It is also important to conduct an inspection to make sure that there is nothing hidden within the property that could result in you losing money. However, if you stick to your guidelines and collaborate with those who are able to handle all legal issues eventually, you'll have an investment in real estate and you can choose what you want take advantage of it in order to make it a profit producer.

Chapter 7: Hiring a Company Versus.

Ad Word and Pay-Per-Click

If you are unable to find the search terms you're looking for or think would be the most efficient in your particular area, by a company such as the one mentioned above it is possible to determine if you are able to purchase the terms you want through AdWords or through Pay-Per-Clicks. I would still suggest hiring an agency to handle both of these since it's more efficient with the time you have and your money. These aren't the same as firms that are similar to World Wide Media and specialize solely in aiding you in managing your AdWords or your Pay-PerClicks rather than selling specific search terms they offer and that only you be the owner of.

The task of managing AdWords managing AdWords Google will be an all-hours task. I did this when I first began my journey and was convinced that I needed an education in AdWords to be able to make the usage of AdWords successful by myself. You must manage the effectiveness of your advertisements and monitor your click-throughs and monitor your maximum bids for every search term to ensure that you encounter someone who has the same phrase but is willing to pay an amount that is higher to be ahead on the list. The list goes on, so trust me when I say it's a more efficient investment of the time, money and effort to let someone else handle this for you.

There are some companies Google has joined forces with and can manage your AdWords on behalf of you. Another benefit of working with a business instead of doing it yourself is that a they can inform you if the phrases or terms you're looking to use are the best choices. They are aware of how often in a month the same phrase is used and will guide you to select the best option available. You can find those companies at WWW.GOOGLE.COM/ADWORDS. On the left there is an option to "get assistance from a certified professional." Select the Search for One Today button.

When using Pay-Per-Clicks, you must set the amount you want to spend , either per day or for a month. The issue with this is that it is possible to blow your budget due to those who are searching are clicking happily. They might click on your advertisement only to click, and then go back to your website. When they return you realize that you've paid for that click but received nothing. Perhaps you'd like to ensure that your website is running properly and conduct your own search to determine the place where your advertisement appears. If you click the ad to ensure that it's on your website and you pay an amount. Keep in mind that with Pay-Per-Click you are charged each when someone clicks on your advertisement and is directed to your website. It isn't important if they click the back button instantly. The click cost you. For search terms, as the user pays a fixed amount to the company responsible for managing your search terms, there's no limit to the number of clicks you will receive and it's the responsibility of the business to ensure that your website appearing at the top of results every single time.

I also noticed that when using Pay-Per-Clicks or AdWords, the quality of leads that be generated were extremely low when compared to paying a business who specialises in managing your terms and keeping your site at the top of the page. The initial two phrases I bought that I could use for my region only cost me

$99.00 for a month, and I can say that I earned an infinity amount of extra money per month from the leads these phrases brought in.

Though you could utilize a mix of keywords, Adwords and Pay-Per-Clicks. I would suggest starting by choosing a business that offers search terms for your location and that has a flat cost. If you're looking to expand your search terms you should find out what search terms are available via AdWords as well as Pay-Per-Click.

To better know how search terms work take a look at the graphic below. There are three sections of the search results page-- areas A, B and C. The first area is where results show through organic search results, which, as I've said is time-consuming and costly to ensure you're in the right area. Area B and C is the places where ads are shown through keywords and is cheaper and, according to me, more efficient. Some might argue the areas B and C aren't as effective as investing thousands of dollars to ensure you come on the internet naturally. I did a search for "dog leashes" in this instance and you will notice that the top two results on the page for Area C, which come higher than the organic sites and is Walmart as well as Amazon. It seems like they consider it beneficial to utilize the search term also.

If you choose the correct keywords and then hire a reputable company that specialises in ensuring that you show first, you will at all times be appearing on the top page and show up in the area B & C.

Specialty Terms

To broaden your reach it is possible to add more terms in the future in order to redirect visitors to your leads capture systems. If, for instance, you are working on a new project that's coming online look up the search terms you want to use are available. If you are in a specific field you'd prefer to focus on, such as ranches or ski properties, river homes, and fishing property Check if these keywords are available. If I stay to my New York Real Estate theme the term that would be a specialty could consist of "Park View Real Estate" or "New York Park Views." It is likely, these niche phrases will be cheaper than the more general ones because they don't have the same volume of people who search for that specific term every month. But, the users who enter the exact term to search for it are more focused on finding what they're looking for than people who are searching for broad terms, and therefore the quality of leads is significantly higher.

Keep in mind that these are search phrases that are not the names of websites. There is no need to purchase 50 websites. When you purchase the keywords, your site is where the users will be directed after they click the link.

Another method of capturing leads is to use a service such as Homegain, Trulia, Zillow, etc. These are web-based companies which specialize in showing on top of the search results in the event that someone is searching for homes in your region. This is a simple way to emphasize my idea. There are websites that earn their profits by appearing as a source of information to look for properties in a particular location. They make use of the same search terms. You can buy from them certain areas, which can fill the gap between search terms that you can purchase from other companies. Perhaps, for instance, you are looking for New York Homes for Sale and the one that charges a flat cost to ensure that your website is listed on the first page doesn't have that option but Homegain has it.

The two sites operate slightly differently and I'll leave it to you to decide, if you have any, which one is the best for your particular area. They don't offer you search terms however, rather, the names of towns, counties zip codes and so on. since that's how you look for properties on their website. I utilize Homegain for my region and should someone visit their site and is searching for properties within my area the person is directed to Homegain's website onto my Lead Capture Page to begin search for properties, and after that I, of course I record their details.

This is a fantastic way to add value to your existing search phrases. Sometimes, I may get two chances instead of just one , if users choose both the Homegain, and maybe one of the terms I bought from another firm.

Chapter 8: Do I Really Need an Agent?

There are three main methods to sell a homethat you can choose from

1. Represented by an agent

22 FSBO (For the Sale of the Owner)

3- Cash sale to investor

In certain transactions, like short sales it is necessary to have an agent. I will go over short sales further in the future. For other equity transactions, using an agent's services can be arranged.

In the process of selling their house, homeowners often consider the commission they pay to an agent as an expense. A few savvy homeowners might think at least 6percent of the home's worth is quite a bit to shell out for putting signs in their yard and moving several documents. However, that's not what you pay an experienced agent to accomplish.

When you employ an agent, you're hiring an expert with extensive expertise in selling homes. You'll want to find someone who is reliable, confident and who has a proven track record of success in sales. Someone who will dedicate themselves to your goals, which include selling your property at the highest value.

As per the National Association of Realtors, more than 80% of properties advertised as FSBO will eventually be registered with an agent and only 8 percent of residential property sales are concluded through for sale by owner transactions. Why is there a huge difference in the numbers?

The main benefits of putting up your property for sale with the help of a Realtor(r) is exposure and security.

A homeowner will typically not be capable of generating the level of exposure that a skilled real estate agent will.

Exposure refers to the amount of advertising that you have done for you, as well as the foot traffic that you generate. Greater exposure will mean more speedy results in finding one potential buyer. The quicker results in finding the buyer will also mean less time spent on house payments in addition.

For instance, if you list your home through an agent, it could take between 30 and 60 days to sell depending on the current market conditions and region. If you sell the home as an FSBO the time could be six to nine months for it to be sold. In the additional 4 to 6 months, you will are liable for carrying expenses. Property taxes, mortgage payments as well as utility bills, and all other costs which continue to accrue are carried expenses. Therefore, if you were forced to pay for the costs for days in markets, FSBO could end up costing you more. Also, In 2015 FSBO houses sold at a rate of 16% less than those that were listed by agents.

In addition to the local MLS the listing of the agent will be distributed across various platforms to increase the national and local attention. Agents have access to the email addresses of all agents in the area. They can contact former clients, investors and collaborate with other agents that already have clients who are looking for homes within your area.

In a matter of days, thousands and millions of people will have heard about your home being put on the market with the assistance of an agent. This is a far greater amount than the number of people who have noticed the sign that you posted placed in front of your property at the end of your cul-de-sac.

For protection purposes When you list with an agent , you will be given state and local disclosures that are designed to shield you as a seller of a home from possible legal action. In addition to the standard Listing Agreement, you will be provided with a list of mandatory disclosures and recommended disclosures that you should fill in and give to the buyer. The disclosures are designed to protect you as the buyer of the transaction. The disclosures are the only important reason to be represented by an Realtor. FSBO transactions are always at danger of not disclosing without proper guidance.

There are certain items that need to be made clear to buyers in a sale transaction. If these items aren't made public, homeowners could open themselves to potential risk. It is not an excuse to not disclose the items and buyers must be aware of their responsibilities before selling their home to safeguard themselves from potential problems.

Agents are also present to help depersonalize the negotiation. A professional isn't going be angry and take it personally when a person makes a poor price or discourteous remarks about the colour that the room has. A homeowner on the contrary side may be offended by comments made about his decor. Agents can stop the ego or any hurt feelings from being a hindrance to the terms and pricing and could even negotiate an agreement with two parties who's personalities aren't compatible.

Selling through an agent can be beneficial for homeowners who need the most exposure to their marketing and security when selling. The homeowner would prefer to be able to have an intermediary handle negotiations. Moreover, the homeowner should expect to receive the highest price when selling.

How to Select an Agent

If you choose to employ the services of an agent for real estate to market your house, you must probably talk to two of them so you can evaluate and contrast.

The agent you choose to work with is basically going serve as your representative. They are acting on your behalf to help you reach your objectives. Price alone isn't an incentive to choose your agent. By "price" I refer to not the commission or charge, but the cost at which they wish to market the property.

You must choose an agent that you believe will be able be able to sell your home within your time frame and at the price that is acceptable to you.

Check if an agent is in real estate full-time or in part-time. If they work on a part-time basis in the business, they might not have knowledge of current trends, marketingtechniques, or the financing choices available to buyers. Additionally, they might not have a reputable group of agents who could have buyers waiting for your home to go on the market.

Some agents charge high in order to obtain the selling price. Beware! A home that is priced too high could result in less buyer interest, more days in marketplace, and instead than helping your home sell, it may help other properties. It is not a good idea to reduce the price, it's not appealing. Make sure you price it right in the beginning by working with the right agent and you will get the results you want.

As you've already decided the worth of your home The first question you should ask you should ask an agent "How much is my house worth?" If the values are in line, you can decide whether the agent is a Realtor(r) (a participant in the National Association of Realtors) or an agent licensed.

Every Realtors(r) have the status of agents, but they are not all Realtors(r). Realtor(r) Realtor(r) is a member of the national Association of Realtors(r) and accepts to conduct business in accordance with the ethical and professional codes set out in the Association. A Realtor(r) has to pay dues to gain access to most current information, classes, declaration forms MLS along with all functions that the NAR(r) offers. It is important to note that the Realtor(r) should also have the status of an agent or broker licensed by the NAR.

The Real Estate agent is licensed with an identical license to Realtor(r) Realtor(r) but has decided not join NAR(r). They may both have the same degree of expertise.

If you decide to engage an agent, bear in mind that YOU are the one who is in charge. This means that the agent is working on behalf of you and should pay attention to your wishes and needs and incorporate them into your overall strategy. If you're a night sleeping person, it's the responsibility of the agent to integrate in the time for viewings to your schedule. It is important to convey your requirements to the agent to ensure that they can be flexible.

If you receive calls from agents on your front yard and ask if they are able to visit your house, even though the directions specifically mention appointment only, don't hesitate to inform them that they require an appointment. If you're unable to attend the day you're hosting a birthday celebration or other event, inform them. It is important to make your home accessible, but you must not feel overwhelmed.

In the end, you'll want to inquire about the marketing strategy of the agent you are considering. Do bigger brokerages always have the most effective results? Some believe that opting to collaborate with an agent who represents the national brand could increase the exposure of their company. I don't agree. In certain situations I think that using a company's name causes the agent to be a somewhat naive. The agent might depend on a sign or ads in newspapers instead of offering full service "full service" that is budgeted into the commission agreed upon with the home owner.

I run the "Boutique brokerage." It is an individual brokeror Realtor(r). I believe that I do more to serve my clients and my services are more personalized and individual. I don't have a full-page ad in the Sunday paper in which your property will be included alongside fifty other properties. Instead, I design for my clients custom marketing strategies that could include specific social media channels and local direct mail and customized marketing to local agents within the region. Of course, I've got experience in marketing, and I put those 25years of experience to use for my clients as well. Brand recognition or name recognition is not at top of my marketing. You won't get that type of service from an agency that is big box My marketing is focused on delivering clients the results they desire, and not to brand my company.

I examine every property I list to determine the potential buyer. I then determine the most effective way to inform the buyer know that his house was just advertised.

I think that the big shotgun strategy is more to aid in the brand name of the brokerage as well as to get more agents on board. I'm not paid to be 1,000 looky-loos to walk around my client's home on Sundays. I am paid to find one buyer who is qualified to submit an offer to purchase the property within a certain time-frame and at a price that is acceptable with my customer.

Instead of placing your home sale in the hands of an organization whose name you know and an agent who might have a strategy for marketing you, you should take the time to talk with agents about the task of selling your house. Learn about the experience and the time and effort that are going to be devoted to the successful sale of your house.

Find out about the marketing strategy. If it is only comprised of placing a sign on your property and then adding your property to the MLS it is possible reconsider your decision of the agent. You should choose an agent whom you believe will sell your house.

Cash Investors

The most efficient method of selling the house is typically selling it for cash in the hands of an investor. This is the most efficient method when speedy sale is more important than everything else.

Most of the time, the cash sales are probate properties or those that are inherited by relatives or even groups. It is more sensible selling quickly to reduce expenses and maintenance for the property which the new owner is unable to afford to pay for.

Sometimes, couples are ordered to liquidate their assets quickly in the event of a pending divorce or a judgment. There may be an imminent bankruptcy and the court order the sale.

Sellers should be willing to put some cash to be left on the table during an instant cash sale however, it isn't essential. The ability to liquidate the asset in a timely manner without any cost to the buyer is the most important thing.

If the property is damaged or has damages or major deferred maintenance, such as roof problems or mold, repairs that are not completed or other repairs, etc. The property might not be eligible for conventional financing. In these situations the buyer will be able to value the property at market value and pay the seller cash within 3-30 days.

Of course , to reap the benefits of a speedy closing and sale in its current condition the buyer is likely be looking for a price reduction for the home. If the buyer is looking to purchase to buy the property for a flip then they'll likely seek a 35 to 55 percent discount on the property to ensure that their calculations are reasonable. If the buyer is a landlord or a real occupant or occupant, the price could be lower. Of course the more work that the property needs, the higher the discount from its fair market value that they would like.

For Sale by the owner FSBO

If time isn't of importance, then you can gamble and try to sell your house FSBO by yourself. This strategy is most effective in a very selling market where the interest in a specific area is greater than the supply.

Many homeowners choose to go the FSBO method since they don't want to decrease their net worth by paying commissions to an agent, as well since they might feel that the agent won't take care of the homeowner in the same way that homeowners be in charge of their own interests.

In the case of buyers, the majority of them realize that an FSBO is not registered with an agent since the owner is trying at saving money. This is why the buyer is likely to lower an offer due to the fact that it is seeking the same type of price reduction. This is why FSBO properties typically sell at a lower price than a traditional selling property with through an agent.

In the majority of cases, when a house is offered by an agent, prospective buyers are screened by their agents and they've got the option of obtaining a loan. This means that agents generally don't present homes to buyers who haven't been approved to buy a house.

The lockboxes that Realtors(r) employ are electronic and every Realtor(r) is assigned a unique code that allows them to access. With this advanced system, it's simple to determine who's at the home, and at what point.

A homeowner must decide if they're going to feel comfortable giving their contact information to the public , and inviting people to an appointment when they show to their door suddenly.

If the FSBO sign is displayed, there are no limitations on who is allowed to take down the number to dial. There could be an increase in calls from telemarketing due to this. The homeowner may also require time to meet with prospective buyers to show them their house. Security and privacy could be a concern when listing the property FSBO.

You'll have to be aware of the disclosure requirements in your local area. homeowners selling their homes might not be familiar with the regulations and laws that govern fair housing as well as lead paint disclosures, and the various other disclosures and laws usually dealt with by your agent. The Realtor(r) is always up-to-date regarding the forms and needed disclosures required for smooth transactions. If you're handling an transaction, you need to be doing the same. The responses to home inspections as well as disclosures to the physical property may become issues.

If there are issues that could arise or issues, it is possible to make price reductions. The last thing that a homeowner would like to risk is an eventual lawsuit due to not disclosing a flaw or other significant fact about the property, the neighborhood or anything that affects any of the. A smart buyer could use problems and omissions to leverage to secure a more substantial price reduction.

An agent who is full-time will be aware of disclosures and inspections, as well as time frames, contingencies, as well as the red flags that lenders raise. It is quite likely that a homeowner will be able to manage everything on their own. They should spend the time to familiarize their self with the procedures but if a problem arises, an FSBO homeowner is solely accountable. Being unaware is not an excuse.

Most buyers are being represented by an agent and knowledgeable agents can assist to bargain the price down until buyers are willing to pay the agent's commission. Sometimes, buyers arrive and be assisted with an agent. If the seller will be willing to contribute a half of the commission to the agent selling You may be able to ask the agent to take care of all disclosures that are required for all sides in the transaction.

A lot of buyers are uneasy about asking questions directly to the homeowner rather than an agent. The homeowner might be emotionally attached to their property and the features they're showing are items you'd want taken away before moving into the property.

The emotions and thoughts can cause problems and it's entirely possible for a home owner to lose a sale before it is written. Inability to communicate is not an issue, especially when there's so much cash at stake.

In the end, the homeowner needs to determine how much of the time he spends is worthwhile. There will be time to set aside for advertising, marketing and scheduling showings, as well as writing the offer signing disclosures, getting signatures and opening the house for inspections and monitoring lenders throughout the process to make sure it is completed in time.

Another option for a FSBO purchase is to seek the assistance by an agent who will provide a lower representation.

Reduced representation can be thought of as the FSBO hybrid. The homeowner will be working with a broker to include a listing in an MLS for a fixed cost. The homeowner will get the most exposure and save cash on the listing aspect of the deal. The homeowner will be responsible for handling all the calls and taking care of negotiations. In some instances, the broker could even offer disclosures that are included in the cost of the flat cost.

There have been instances when homeowners just needed help or someone to go over the documents. I was able to help without much effort by me. The homeowners could have someone experienced in the field review the documents and provide the required information.

There should be a written contract between the broker and homeowner that states that the broker will provide only documents, and the homeowner represents himself. In actuality every Real Estate agreements must be written down to avoid confusion later.

To maximize exposure and protection from disclosures ensure that you hire an agent with experience in marketing who can develop and implement a strategy to sell your house. If you work with an agent and a professional, you will earn the highest net profit from the sale. You can sell the property as an owner-owned for sale (FSBO) in the event that you are not sure about agents and the market is crowded with a small quantity of homes. If you are in need of to liquidate your property quickly, you can sell the house to a cash investor the condition it is in. Be aware that when you sell to investors, you are making money but it may be worth more than the need for cash at present.

Chapter 9: Do's and Don'ts of investing

There are many mistakes to be made when real estate investment to the point where you could lose your entire initial capital along with your house and other property. What are the reasons to put yourself in this precarious situation? You can guard yourself from the most basic errors of investing by making sure you are aware of what they are. Being forewarned will help you stay clear of the most common errors.

There's one thing you must do now. This sounds like a command that is not an appropriate way to communicate however, there's a valid reason to follow this. It is time to stop looking for the magic of the real estate market. No matter what books you've read and the seminars you've attended, or the stories you've heard -- you should stop looking for the magic.

The only way to ensure that nothing happens when it comes to making money is through hard work. It's not by following the formula of someone else's to success or relying on their luck. Let's look at the various seminars available there.

They travel to every city across the USA and bring in those that are looking to learn more about investing in real estate. It could be about rentals Fix and Flips, as well as investment companies. The instructor will tell you to make a personal check that's worth $1 million and then put the date. You're awed by these sessions due to the language used and the excitement.

It isn't common to find greater than one percent attendees to be able to earn their million. What's the reason? because the formula and details you receive are not likely to be appropriate for every one of your. What works in a marketplace located in Denver, Colorado is highly unlikely to be successful with Los Angeles, California. This is the reasons for providing general advice in every section of this book . It can help you determine ways to begin your own business based on your requirements and your capital requirements and the degree of involvement.

The more you believe that you can make money from "magic" properties transactions the longer it's going to take to earn money from real estate. Here are ten more "Don'ts" to keep in mind and keep you on the right path.

Do not plan ahead.

Do not think of investing in real estate as a way to get wealthy quick.

Don't be the only one to invest.

Do not pay too much

Do not skip the investigation

Don't forget to do your due diligence

Don't be fooled by the cash flow

Make sure you have an exit strategy

Don't make a mistake with your amount of time and money.

Do not try to make the sale

Do not plan ahead.

Before you invest in your very first residential real estate transaction You must have a strategy. The plan should determine the highest amount you're willing to pay. Be aware of the saying "if it doesn't come effortlessly, it's not intended to be." There are plenty of fantastic real estate deals that have come on the market, but often they're not intended to become yours.

One of the best examples is a home that can be repaired and then flipped. The smart investors were considering the property as a possible home for a time after they had it fixed and would offer it for sale when the market began to grow in the region. However there was a series of events that caused the deal to be a disaster. The investors had to provide for their families and friends, so it was good they weren't tied to an undertaking that would have taken a lot of time.

It could seem like luck or fate It may sound like luck or destiny, but it's normal to apply the laws of averages. When something is more difficult to attain, there's an explanation for why it's not working out as well.

Instead of trying to convince yourself of things that aren't in your strategy, turn away. If a property is available for sale for $128,000 , and you have a maximum of $130,000, including real estate costs Don't exceed that number.

Consider the potential value rise and the possibility of a situation that could result in more cost than you anticipated. If, for instance, you're purchasing a house for rental What could be the cause of the rent within the initial year? Do you have to repair the roof, flooring as well as the stove, water heater or any other appliance?

Always keep a written plan in place to review your plan and plan for every situation you can control by knowing what might happen.

Do not think of investing in real estate as a way to get quick riches.

There are people who have made it rich quickly through real estate investments. They're portion of the very small number of successful cases. A majority of people are earning modest earnings from real property investments. They build up their retirement accounts or enjoy a luxurious holiday with the cash they've made. There's such a thing as a market that is becoming overcrowded, not just with homes to be sold as well as investors. Take a look at how subprime loans are affecting the market.

This was the time when the property value was too highand excessive loans were made to properties that were overvalued, and people were not able to pay back their loans. As foreclosures began to take place and the market became flooded with properties that were unable to be sold. Retail outlets began to go under and people who were part of real estate investment organizations were losing money due to having to pay for rent that was not paid. The market could turn against you , or hold back a lucrative income. Don't make the mistake of thinking that the real estate investing is a fast-track to riches idea.

Don't be the sole investor

It's great to be the sole investor. You can keep the profits to you. You also have control over the investment. But, it could very harmful on your investment savings. In a matter of seconds it is possible to completely lose your investment. There are investors who invest on their own. They have had success and don't think that this means it can't be accomplished. But, it's cautionary against putting all your money in one investment, and being the only one with that investment. The variety of possible things that could be wrong could lead to financial problems. When you are investing with another investor it is possible of investing less savings, but having more time to make the return you expected from your investment, or at the very least getting to break even.

This is a great rule of thumb for those who don't have a solid understanding of the subject or are new to the field. When you are more experienced in real estate investing it is possible that you will discover there are "sure" offers that are worth making the investment on your own. These are not uncommon however, it's an excellent idea to be among the three or two investors in the event that the market is skewed against you. A subprime-related mortgage meltdown as well as the resultant influx of homes to rent or sell can be a valuable lesson on the reasons why you should be partnering for investing in real property.

Don't be too stingy with your money.

You must be able to pay wholesale rates for the property you invest in specifically when you are investing in an investment property for rental or an existing home to sell. When you invest in REITs or real estate investment companies, you are typically not in control of the price for the purchase. However, this doesn't mean that you have to go out and pay what is requested. There are many deals in the marketplace. It is not necessary to invest into the first deal that appears. It is possible to wait to determine if there's an investment opportunity better.

The principal rule here is to only take what your capital says is appropriate. In the event that you've got $50 of savings and want to invest $25,000, you should not sign up for deals that make your savings disappear. There is also an issue of overpaying for REITs or real estate investment organizations in order to generate profits and sell an investment is not earning money. For instance, let's say you're asked to purchase a REIT which is a casino that is trying to segregate the land from their buildings. They're doing this to obtain tax advantages and also to recover the money they have earned to fund their casino. The amount of money they invest in this case may be too large.

Do not skip the research

The cost of paying too much is frequently an issue when it comes to research. If you do not conduct study, it is likely that you will to overlook something crucial regarding the purchase. You may find that you do not miss any thing, but in the majority of situations, you'll end getting caught out. There are many scams in the world of real estate. Doing your homework wrong could put you in being entangled in.

Additionally, you may purchase a house at wholesale but later find out that it is not possible to sell it as there is something not correct regarding the property. There are, naturally many scenarios or "could be" scenarios that can be mentioned in this article. Instead of boreing you with all these scenarios, consider the situation with common sensible. If you do not conduct researching, you're in danger of getting into problems, rather than doing your research and making a wise choice.

Don't forget to do your due diligence

Due diligence is a different concept that focuses on research, but it also encompasses numerous other aspects of investing in real estate. It is important to do the investigation of the property the deal, real estate investment or REIT provided. Don't not look into the individuals who run the business and selling the property or who are involved with the investments.

A REIT's purpose is to ensure that everyone does not have 50 percent of the trust, however, there are instances where someone is buying to gain more shares. Someone might be seeking to get an advantage through having specific investors backing them and thus, they are the ultimate decision regarding the way the company runs the REIT.

There are stories to be told and theories can be created. The most important thing is to conduct your research so that you are aware of who is involved in the REIT, the length of time the REIT has been operating for, or the number of people who are investing in real estate companies. The more details you're equipped with, such as the way rent income, dividends or day-to-day operations is managed, the better you will be able to make an informed choice about which investment opportunity to profit from.

Don't make assumptions about the flow of cash

You can use two methods to miss the cash flow. You could mistakenly estimate the amount of cash you'll receive from renting a property or change the property and fix it. In this scenario you are accountable for the loan or the return of your investment. You may have believed that you had a tenant who will stay for 10 years. It is possible that you entered into a contract where you believed you could sell the house within three months, only to discover that you've been sat in the property for 12 years due to the fact that you are unable to complete the renovations. There are a variety of ways that you could misread the flow of cash. Certain aspects are yours to manage, while others you can't. In the case of things you control it is essential to manage your finances in a way that is efficient. Don't leave and spend your rent money believing that it will be returned to you at the right time to pay an installment on your mortgage.

In the case of real estate investment groups and REITs Cash flow is all about the amount of money the trust or group has and how they plan to invest in it, and how they can earn a profit from the investment. You must analyze the trust's or group's financials through an analysis of their finances. Review the reports from the periods of lean and also the pertinent year. It is important to determine how the business handles the economic crisis and also the performance they have had in the past two years. These are all great indicators of a proper cash flow.

Do not forget to create an exit strategy

The term "exit strategy" is that is commonly used in the investment world that include REITs hedge funds, mutual funds and stocks. But, it is applicable to any real estate investment. A strategy for exit is how to exit from an investment when it's not performing well and also how to exit it in the first place.

That's where all the amount of planning that you make comes into play. There will be an entry strategy, which means you will have a price that you're looking to invest at. If you are looking to fix and flipproperty, then there are renovation costs to think about along with the amount of time is required to complete the renovations done. Also, you have a plan in place to sell the house once the repairs are completed. It is essential to have a strategy like this for all your investments, including a variety of options for exiting based on how the real estate market will shift.

It is important to note that the real estate industry isn't as commonplace as other investments. In one day, a company can lose $100, yet make it back and more than that, meaning you're up by $100 over three days. In the case of real estate, the market is influenced by each purchase or not-purchase. It also alters in response to major economic changes like an increase in inflation, a rise in interest rates, or an election.

It is best to have a plan of escape for every situation, even the things you can't predict. It is ideal having a crystal ball but nobody knows the future. It is possible to research or listen to experts look at your market and attempt to anticipate how it might change over the months ahead while you're investing into your deal. It could be the same which allows your ideal exit strategy to work.

Do not miscalculate the amount of timing and the amount of money.

In the main this "don't" is mostly associated with situations where you can fix and flip. However, it could also be a reminder to be aware of any real estate investments that you undertake. As mentioned above it is important to have a strategy with an exit strategy. It is possible to end up in a difficult situation in the event that you do not calculate the amount of time and the amount required to fund the investment. In the case of REITs, you're not expected to ask for more money, however you could find that it hard to get out of the deal if you don't know the time frame for selling out from the fund. It can also be possible to under estimate the profits you could earn because you are not aware of the taxes you need to be paying or about the sum that you will receive in dividends.

If you are considering fix and flips you'll want to double what you believe the amount of time and money it will take to fix the property up and then sold. When it comes to rentals, the amount of time and cash flow will be determined when you consider the time it will be to rent the property as well as how much you'll have to invest in advertising, and what you could charge for the rental property.

Do not try to make an offer

There are instances where you can spot an opportunity to profit from an area or a an area of land. It has the potential. However, the owner might not want to sell the property or at least at a price that is suitable to your financial investment. This is the time you must cut and run. Don't try to force an offer with the seller. It is possible that they have to sell due to a variety of reasons, some of which are dire ones. Eventually, they'll be forced to sell at a price that is yours. But, if you pressure for them to sell, and do it now, they won't ever sell "ever," at least to you. Sometimes , people know what needs to be done, but they must to wait for their time before they get to the point of selling. In other situations there may not be a need to sell, and forcing a sale isn't going to be successful.

The opposite can be stated as "don't try to coerce someone to purchase." If this is the scenario don't buy an item and attempt to convince others to purchase it once it's ready to sell. You must advertise the property. It is important to highlight the advantages and must have open houses in order to allow people to tour the property. But, you don't need to appear overly aggressive or desperate when you attempt to sell a home.

People should consider whether it's their belief that they will be at home and content by what it offers instead of what you think it will provide to offer them.

The list of errors or "Don'ts" is a generalization and will provide you with an understanding of errors that you could make when you go deeper into the specific tips that pertain to four primary kinds of investments. Consider these "Don'ts" while you go through the various types of investment and consider which investment is best to suit your needs based upon the amount of time you are willing to invest and the capital you have to start with as well as the risk and the rewards you'll gain.

Chapter 10: Nuts And Bolts

If you're not making calls to prospects and aren't taking phone calls on the floor, and not asking your friends or family members for recommendations, then what do you do to find lists?

My approach has been a blessing for my business as I've said previously. It's the least intrusive method of make a sale, and it offers benefits to the customer. Doesn't it sound like it's too promising to be real? It's not true. It worked for me and it could be a success for you too. Let's take a look at all the nuts and bolts that make up this process.

My approach involves the use of printed communications with the prospective client. A carefully designed and tested letter starts the process. The manner that it is presented creates a unique experience and appealing to the buyer. The letter is followed by a sequence of seven postcards, which are mailed to the recipient every 3 days.

My experience is that most times, I received a call before I had sent my third, or even fourth card and didn't have to send any more.

The receipt of a letter from the post office that begs to be read and is less intrusive and considerate of someone's interest and. I am sure that I would prefer to receive an informative and thoughtful letter rather than having my phone ringing constantly.

Also, the moment a seller's listing expires, phone calls immediately begin. They're bombarded by realtors who are repeating the same message repeatedly. Most likely, the seller will be completely avoiding answering the phone. Today, many people don't even answer the phone when they are unable to know the number. This makes it extremely difficult to reach an actual person on the line even when you try.

My approach allows the buyer to open the letter and take a look, or set it for later, when they are able to read it. Or, of course, dispose of it. Whatever decision you make to go with, your odds of them reading my letter are higher than making them contact me via my phone but also getting them to schedule an appointment with me.

Let's start by addressing the correspondence. We'll go over the contents of the letter in the next few minutes, but before that I'd like to go over the specific manner in which the letter, along with the postcards should be prepared and handed out.

I will always place the two-page letter as well as the testimonial page into an 8x11 envelope. And, it is crucial I write their name and address, as well as my return details. I don't utilize labels and do not write "To the homeowner". I make sure to verify their name in tax documents.

Take a moment to think about this for a minute. If you received a written envelope that measured 8x11 Would you throw it in the garbage without even ever opening it? I doubt it. A huge envelope with an address that is personal and handwritten with a return address is just too appealing to discard.

For an address to return I will always include:

My Full Name

My full address for my office and zip code

There is no company name It's not a company name! They might be more likely to throw it away when they are aware that it is being supplied by XYZ Real Estate!

The letter should be personalised to be specific to you. I recommend that you don't alter the contents, unless you absolutely need to. This letter was written and revised by me over the course of trying various variations over the many years. This particular letter is the one that has gotten the best results. Save the link and open this document. This is your chance to grow your business beyond what you could ever imagine!

Click Here to Be Taken to the Letter That's Expired

After having read the letter, I'd like to discuss the postcards. Sending a letter is the best way to begin but it is important to be consistent. There must be an additional follow-up. That's where postcards are useful.

After three days have passed since I delivered the mail, I send postcard number one. Every 3 days I mail the next postcard. It is crucial to distribute them in this manner. The recipients will be able to recognize the logo and could be tempted to think this realtor has been around for a while. There are always sellers who are unhappy, but at the very the very least, they will be able to throw your letter. It's not like you are calling them out of the blue like many of other realtors who might try to contact them. Click on each link below to open the postcards.

Postcard #1Postcard #5

Postcard #2 Postcard #6

Postcard #3Postcard #7

Postcard #4

I hope that they'll be like the majority of homeowners. If they've not decided to sell their home with their previous agent, or to take the time to think about how they can sell, they'll contact you. Perhaps it's because of the assurance (which I'll describe in the next post) and their interest in the guarantee. Perhaps it's the persistance on the cards. Perhaps it's something about the postcards or letters that enticed them. No matter what the cause, if you enjoy the things they see, they will contact you instead of the opposite. You have a buyer who has shown that they're very attracted. Aren't they the most desirable kind of buyers?

A few points about the design and format of the postcards and letterheads. Note that there are a few shades of color incorporated into specific words in the text. Don't overdo it. Make sure to stick with this style. It's attractive without too dominant. If you are using too much red, for instance it will lose its power. You might want to consider adding red chili powder to recipes. It's a great flavor and spice, but too much can ruin the flavor of the dish!

It is also essential to keep a consistent graphics and fonts. Similar to the colors, you should not use too many graphics. Be simple enough that people are drawn to the content , and don't distract the reader with too many images and cutesy things. Maintain this consistent style on the postcards. You want your readers to be able to recognize these documents as being uniquely yours.

For graphics you can think of a simple graphic at the top right area of your letter or perhaps your company's logo. Feel free to include an image of yourself in the lower left corner should you wish to.

Sellers prefer to include an image with a name and this is an ideal option. But, I would like to add that your picture should be placed at the bottom, not right at the top. This is not about your self-esteem. It's about giving the buyer a glimpse your personality.

Whatever your design or logo, make sure to keep it neat and clean. I think the font that I've designed is appealing to the eyes. This is what you are looking for. Overly cluttered images and the excessive use of bold print, italics as well as... aren't the best ideas.

After we've gone over the format of the documents we can now take a few minutes to talk about the most important aspect... that hook!

The Hook

Okay So "the Hook" sounds so negative. It's almost commercial... is it even a word? However, there must be something that can distinguish you from all the other realtors that will try to reach out to the seller within a few days after their listing is expired.

In conclusion, I want to be clear, real estate isn't brain surgery. Do we not all do similar things? Put your home on the MLS Advertise via various web sites, organize open houses, etc...

What could we do to set us from the rest? It's a good question. .... We could even offer to purchase their house even if they don't want to sell. I don't know about your but I've never had several hundred thousand dollars lying around to accomplish this.

We might offer to sit at the corner in an outfit of a clown holding a sign with the address of their house all day on Saturday.

We could host open houses with realtors, in which we served champagne, snacks, and there was a violinist who played on the side.

We could place an ad of one page in the front in the paper.

The list could go on. However, there's something we can do to set ourselves apart. We can provide them with an opportunity to have their home sell.

Did you blink your eyes? I noticed that!

I'm serious about this. Think about this. If I purchase an item or product, I will always search for an assurance. If I invest $200 in a blender that is top of the line I'd should have a warranty that I'll receive my money back in the event that it does not work. Wouldn't it be fair?

If people decide to hire us to market their home and trust that we'll sell the property. Wouldn't it be great for business should we offer the buyers a guarantee?

Here's the point. I do not charge fees in advance. The majority of realtors don't either. If a seller does not take a single penny in advance What does it mean to be a "guarantee? We aren't able to "refund" the amount they've never received.

That leads our attention to the fundamentals and nuts of this system is about. THE GUARANTEE.

Chapter 11: Bankruptcy

In some states , a real estate investor may purchase an item known as"the "post-bankruptcy listing." A post-bankruptcy listing includes the names, addresses and, sometimes, the telephone numbers of those who have tried to prevent their houses from going into default by filing bankruptcy. If your state doesn't have a vendor that will offer you a post-bankruptcy listing, you can make one yourself through a subscription to Pacer. Locate a legal professional who has worked with real estate lawyers and/or bankruptcy lawyers. Spend an hour of her time to help you through the process of using Pacer to locate real homeowners who have been exiled from bankruptcy. For locating a legal professional post an advertisement on Craigslist or sign up to a big church and inform everyone that you're in search of an attorney that requires some extra time.

When a homeowner is forced to the expense and effort to hire a bankruptcy lawyer to file for bankruptcy in order to save his house, he believes that he's accomplished everything possible to do so there's often a huge feeling of peace and calm that isn't present in other motivated sellers. Most of the time, a seller who has declared bankruptcy will smile wide at you, wave and then say "Thank for your help for your help, but everything is taken into consideration!" The homeowner really believes that everything is fine, however this is not always the scenario. To truly protect the home from foreclosure , the homeowner has to follow the court's guidelines for repaying the debts, and the issue is always the income. If there is no work or a spouse who is sick, the homeowner will usually be in a position to not be able to follow the bankruptcy rules of the court and mortgage holders are typically able to have the foreclosure process restarted. The foreclosure notices could start appearing again, however the homeowner believes that it's a error because he filed for bankruptcy, and believes that he has taken charge of everything. They're in denial, and could be surprised when they are removed from their property due to a foreclosure taking place. I am sure that their bankruptcy attorney tried all he could in explaining the procedure however, most sellers aren't aware of the business.

If you truly want to pursue sellers motivated by their desire who were thrown out of bankruptcy due to their inability to adhere to the bankruptcy rules, act with a lot of compassion. Try sending an array of letters to are polite and straightforwardly clarify that from public records that their home has been being rescheduled for foreclosure due to their inability to adhere to this bankruptcy program. If you are able to fill your letter with compassion and kindness , and then send each week and so on, you might receive a phone call.

The majority of people aren't entrepreneurs and have no idea how to begin a new business, or want to create a business. If the job they have lost, and after that, their spouse loses their job, they're in serious trouble. There are a lot of people who are worried about the prospect of having to live with family members they don't like or perhaps reside in a shabby hotel. Pre-foreclosures don't say this, but this is the way they think. Though it's never occurred to me, I wouldn't have been shocked to hear that a pre-foreclosure-motivated seller was crying in tears. I've had other residential investors share their stories about having to collect motivated sellers and take to the closing. They're not as mentally ill but disabled by fear.

Take Care!

If you've a better understanding of the motivations of sellers such, it's essential to consider how you can safeguard yourself. If you've got money to invest in licensing and technology then you'll be more secure and more satisfied. If you're in a tight financial situation, you can still stay safe by following a few simple steps.

First, get your real estate salespersons license. If you continue to engage in investing in residential real estate, I am sure you'll eventually meet an angry, vengeful client who will take every step to make you uncomfortable. The most efficient and cost-effective method to achieve this is to charge you with operating in real estate without having a license. If this happens you have the option to defend yourself, or employ an attorney that could cost you thousands of dollars. If you attempt to defend yourself against the charge , and fall short, the punishment could be several thousand dollars.

The cost of licensing isn't cheap, but it's a sensible choice. In the end, you'll come over a buyer who is better off by listing their property with an agent since they are not in a hurry to sell. In this case you may offer to sell the property for your client as his agent. You will earn a commission, and you could end having to pay for your license course and exam. There is a good chance that motivated sellers face issues with real estate agents , so you'll need practice in the two roles. It is likely that you will need inform your client that you're licensed as an agent in the beginning however you are able to explain to them that your state requires that you be licensed, and you're playing the role of an investor to his property as well as his owner. It is sometimes difficult to find investment properties that are good in certain instances, and the revenue that your license can generate can be extremely beneficial.

If you start your home-based investing career with an agent's license for real estate salesperson it is a massive weapon away from an angry frustrated, angry seller. If you don't have that weapon, the seller could complain to your broker, so it's crucial to choose an agent who is open to investors, and most importantly one who is an investor. When your broker is experienced and has dealt with sellers who are motivated and knows how they can behave. If you're an investor of a female gender, I suggest an investor-friendly broker who is like a linebacker from the NFL. A sour-faced seller might visit the office, discuss his alleged grievances to your broker , and then disappear. Do your research and look up brokers in depth until you're certain that you have located an investor-friendly broker who will help and protect you.

Certain residential real estate investors hesitate to register as agents due to the fact that they are aware or think that a broker might not permit the investor to use their sales contract. A broker might insist that you utilize the standard contract for sales in real estate used by all state agents have to use in lieu of yours. An investor might be hesitant due to the fact that there are clauses in the contract that are crucial for her investment. This issue can generally be resolved with an addition for the existing contract following an interview with the real estate lawyer of your broker. One reason your broker is attempting to utilize the typical real estate sale agreement is so that he can keep the state's real estate agent commission from his pocket and out of his pocket, and this is a good objective.

When you've met the lawyer of your broker who is an investor friend, it is advisable to ask him for guidance on running your investing company as a limited-liability business. When you're operating as an agent for real estate and broker, you'll be covered by errors or omissions insurance, which will protect your losses in the event that you fail to make a mistake in the course of a transaction. To protect yourself when acting as an investor in real estate you'll have to establish the proper legal entity and operate solely under the name of this organization. This is especially important considering the sometimes agitated and insensitive nature of the seller who is motivated. There is a good chance to find that the broker you choose will be acquiescent to you implementing whatever strategy his real estate attorney recommends. The attorney of your broker may be able to direct your to an insurance broker who could offer you a contract of insurance which will protect you for the actions of an investor in real estate.

Certain real estate agents possess an "us to them" mentality toward residential investors. Before I was authorized as an agent, I was often shocked with the hostile attitude I experienced from real estate agents. To put it simply the real estate agents believed the notion that I was a fraud and they made this obvious to me, and even at my side. It was in spite of having many many years of expertise in the field of real estate investment and also a master's education in the field of business. When they came to understand me and realized I was legitimate and legitimate, I received a little more respect however it was too late. The damage had already been accomplished. Real estate brokers and agents are a influential political lobby, and that industry is in majority of the time, hostile to investor. They view the most innovative home real estate buyers particularly, as opponents and instruct their agents and brokers to offer unlicensed buyers the cold shoulder, at minimum. Be prepared by the fact that an agent is able to file a complaint by the real estate commissioner of your state for attempting to practice real estate without an authorization. Whyis that? In simple terms Real estate agents are concerned that illegal creative investors take their businesses.

A way to stay clear of resentment of real estate professionals is to get licensed and sure that the broker you choose is a good investor. Find out if your potential broker is a real estate investor himself, and what his preferred investment strategies are. I could tell that my broker was aware of the characteristics of motivated sellers like when he shared his personal war story. It appears that my broker, who is an experienced real estate broker and investor was selling the property and was not part of the title chain, i.e. that he was not the owner of that parcel of land. This is the essence of the licensing law. The real estate salesperson's licence gives you the legal authority to sell real estate you've never owned. It seems that someone thought my broker was committing an act of con-artistry and contacted his FBI on him. This was, looking back, found hilarious. Many things are hilarious when you look back. My personal belief is that the informant contacted the commission on real estate first , but the commission ignored his call when they found out his broker's license. Unwilling to concede this easily, he made a call to the FBI.

It is important to consider gender and there are particular requirements specifically for women investors. An investor who is female must consider what she'd do if she visited the property of an impulsive seller and something was horribly wrong. It's never occurred to me, but in the course of my career, which spans years, something awful could occur. Realtors have been sexually assaulted and killed during their profession simply having a conversation with men to show him a home. It could happen to a female investor too , and if warned is prepared.

If you're registered as an agent, then it is essential to ensure that the office you work for knows the place you'll be on an appointment as well as who you'll be getting to know. If you're not a licensed agent you should attempt to take a male companion or your husband to appointments to meet with male-motivated sellers. If that's not feasible make sure at least one and at a minimum two people knows where you're traveling to and whom you will be meeting. I have a pendant for emergency 911 in my neck and beneath my clothing to be able to press a button to call 911 at any moment. I think this is an excellent option for women who invest. One less costly, but more innovative option is to keep your cell phone in your pocket or purse make a call to an acquaintance or friend, then switch the phone to speaker mode and allow the caller to listen to the conversation until you're safe in your vehicle. In addition, firearms is able to put in your bag if you are carrying an authorization to carry concealed. It's not pleasant to think about the possible negative consequences that can happen when you're in a room with someone you've have just met, but it's more beneficial to think about them and plan for them before you be the victim of an attack.

If you're certain you'll be dealing with an individual selling retail, then I believe it's okay to dress in your typical formal outfit. If however, you are certain that you will be dealing with a salesperson who is motivated I recommend dressing more casually. You can wear a long-sleeved t-shirt even in summer. It's only going to be a view of the house for a few minutes or so, and you will be able to endure the temperatures. Long sleeves can shield your from the apprehension of big mosquitos, horse flies, and maybe rats and bats. I recommend blue jeans tucked into water-proof, sturdy work boots that extend to your knee. If you fall onto a nail that is rusty I'm sure the sole of your boots will stop it from reaching your foot. However, a tetanus booster shot prior to beginning your investment is as safe in the same way as getting a real-estate permit. Work gloves made of leather are an excellent idea. After careful planning of consideration, thought, and instruction, you are able to carry a concealed gun within your wallet or bag. It is recommended to carry at least one high-powered flashlight in your trunk, and I suggest two. You can keep one in your trunk or hand it over to the seller who is motivated and then take one along with you. A lot of these homes are without power source. Also, I highly recommend the use of bug repellent on exposed skin.

When you leave the home be sure to check for ticks and spiders. Walking through a house that has been abandoned for a long time is a frightening experience, but make detailed observations on the lead sheets, and take photos.

Chapter 12: Why You Should Purchase A Home While You're Young

1. INVESTMENT

Real estate is an excellent investment option. If you can legitimately own a house during your 20s and then rent it out to your coworkers in exchange for their payment the rent, you'll be using the rent to pay for your mortgage.

2. APPRECIATION

It is also crucial to remember that the earlier you buy a house, the longer it will take to increase in value. The annually appreciated value of a property that is located in a good location could be in the range of 15% to 20 percent. This can result in an enormous increment in the value of investment for such an asset.

It also makes more sense to invest your hard-earned money in a rising asset, instead of paying monthly rental with none at all.

3. RETURN on Investment

The return you'll earn on your investment can't be compared with any value in the near future. I have a home I purchased for N275,000 in 2009, and today the same property is available at N4.7 million.

4. ACCOUNT FOR CUSTOM SAVINGS

Inscribing your money in the construction of an investment property is Savings and, just like you are able to quickly withdraw funds in your savings accounts you could also earn cash from the property through rental or even reselling it.

Another benefit of buying an early-life home is the fact that it's more affordable to pay for recurring expenses with savings that accumulate later on in the course of. Also, it opens the possibility of upgrading to a larger, more centrally located house in the near future.

5. In the event of a rental income

You can earn income by using rental services. Renting out all or a part of your home automatically generates an income stream for you.

6. Creativity

A house purchase is an expression of your creativity. It's not easy to adhere to the rules necessary to build a home.

7. RESPONSIBILITY/FREEDOM

A house that is built early is the responsibilities. Also, it frees you from the burden of yearly rents and the repression of landlords.

8. CONCEPT OF THE FINANCE

One Naira today will never be one tomorrow. The value of money varies as time passes. I was told about one man who built an house in the 80's , and called his house "Adebowale House". His friends who received the same amount of money as he received, purchased automobiles and enjoyed luxurious lifestyles. The value of these cars diminished over time, but this house still stands. Amazingly, he is now earning more money from his home than he did back in the 1980's.

9. FREE TIME

If you build a house as a child, you've put in the time and your future is secure for you.

10. COLLATERAL FOR BETTER SUBSTANTIES

Any thing you create could be utilized as collateral at any point. If you have to start an enterprise which requires a substantial amount however, banks might not be able to lend you money unless you have collateral.

11. Upgrade of ENVIRONMENT to live a better life

A friend of mine had approximately the same number of houses within Agege however, she was planning to purchase a house located in Banana Island. In order to achieve her aim, she sold smaller houses in Agege as well as one house in Ikeja. It was simple to raise the cash because she already had properties.

Chapter 13: Wireframing the Motivation of Sellers

Questions: "Well John, it seems like a great location (pause for a moment to think about the words he used) However, why do you want to sell it?

Rationale:

If there is no reason to buy, the query will help you in determining the motive behind selling is and reduce the conversation. In general, sellers will bring up something that makes the conversation appear from the perspective of a person's viewpoint and often respond as if they're in bankruptcy or engaged in divorce, or simply want to sell rather than fix it. You, as an investor, must be aware of the subtle shift in tone of the voice of the seller back to one that is motivated who's goal is to get the property sold quickly and quickly.

There is no need to make use of it, but rather take it in a respectful manner toward the vendor. These subtleties are utilized to subconsciously inform the seller that the price of the property might not be the only factor when selling it, however, at the same the seller may realize that the main factor in the issue is to sell quickly and quickly. The price and discussion gets put back in the right perspective, without you discussing the cost or any other way. In any event you could say something things like: "Well, we really do not care about whether we sell it or don't" however, you must quickly realize that the sellers aren't motivated in any way; then you're free to move on with the next vendor.

Practice your negotiation on the phone and pre-screening other potential sellers could improve your manner of communicating, and help you understand more about the motivations of sellers or lack of. Sometimes, you will have to work with different inheritors but the incentive to sell isn't high because they don't like the idea of splitting the profits. Consider this scenario: There are four inheritors, and the net amount after sale is around 80K, which is 20K per each. You can help the beneficiaries to pay an appropriate price by describing the net proceeds in four pieces, such as telling them, "What I can offer is 15 thousand dollars for each beneficiary after the closing". But you must make this statement slowly and with no any pretense. Be aware that you need to know everything about how to communicate in a conversation.

At this point, sellers will be aware that your offer is lower than the price they were looking for initially, and you must approach the issue from a more personal view. Furthermore, receiving a reduction of 5K than a week's the sale will sound more convincing. This will certainly aid them in avoiding misperception and get a more unreasonable prices for sale. Instead, they should start to remember why they should make the decision to sell their property in the initial instance. If you are certain that you are one of them you could play your cards out.

Questions: "How much do you have to pay for the John?" or "What's due on the debt John?"

Rationale:

It is essential to make sure you ask the question in an empathetic and low tone of voice that indicates an interest. Your goal is to engage with your sellers on their comfort level with the conversation. However, the questions could be confusing for sellers, which is why they might be experiencing anxiety. What you need to do is allow them to trust you and feel at ease with you and they will do what you would like. It is possible to start by being honest and professional focused on the situation, as well as making sure your tone and manner to be friendly.

It is essential to maintain a professional attitude whenever you can to prevent you from overstepping the line in order to avoid the risk of a potentially dangerous situation. Do not be too friendly or too relaxed, as they might request more than is necessary in the particular circumstance. In addition to paying attention to their needs and showing compassion it is essential to keep a healthy balance between being a professional and remain objective to be able to negotiate professionally and close the deal.

Chapter 14: What are the Payment Methods I Have?

When you get your money from a reverse mortgage you can choose a lump sum, or monthly payments that are the same each month, arranged as a credit line or a combination of each of these. Discuss your individual desires and needs with the bank that issued the reverse mortgage in order to decide which option is best for you.

How much would I get?

Based on your age (or your age if you are your most youthful spouse when there's two of them) and the appraisal value for your house, current rates of interest and the loan limit of the loan type you select the loan limit can differ greatly. The older you get as well as the more valuable your home is can be, the greater the amount you could receive.

Are there restrictions on how I can use this money?

There are no limitations regarding how you may make use of the funds of your reverse loan. The majority of the time, they are used to cover monthly costs of living, but they can even be employed to cover healthcare expenses or pay off debt. Reverse mortgage funds can be utilized at the discretion of the homeowner.

What is the rate of interest on reverse mortgages?

The interest is only charged on the amount you've drawn. The interest will increase until the loan is due at which point the interest is due in the full amount. Fixed rates as well as adjustable rates are provided. It is recommended to speak with several lenders and then compare rates of interest as well as the costs for the loan.

When will the loan become due?

The reverse mortgage is due then the principal (plus interest, and any upfront closing costs that were not paid when the loan was placed in place) is due in the event that it is one of the following events occurs:

If the person who borrowed the money (1) is killed, (2) sells the property or (3) ceases to live in the house (check the lender's guidelines for duration of time permitted).

If the borrower is living in the house, the borrower isn't obliged to make monthly payments to the balance of the loan.

If a couple is applying for a mortgage it is required to ensure that at minimum one person is living in the house as their primary residence and keeps the house in conformity with FHA guidelines. The insurance and taxes also have to be current. If all requirements are met the loan will not be due.

What are the requirements I have to fulfill to qualify for the reverse-mortgage?

This loan option is that is specifically designed for seniors. The current requirements are as the following:

* You (or the youngest spouse in the case of an unmarried couple) must have at least 62 of age.

* You must be the owner of the property in full or have substantial equity.

* You must reside on the house as your main residence.

* You are not in default on any federal debt.

* You must take part in a counseling session for consumers delivered by a HUD certified HECM counselor.

Beginning on April 27 in 2015, the lender will begin conducting an assessment of the financial situation of each borrower who has a reverse mortgage to make sure that the borrower is financially able to pay for mandatory obligations (such as homeowner's insurance or property taxes) as specified in the loan contract.

The lenders will look at all sources of income like pensions as well as social Security, IRAs and 401K plans, in addition to the credit history of the individual. They will also take a look at the amount of money available to homeowners after the typical expenses are paid monthly. Borrowers must provide documents like tax returns as well as bank account statements to be considered for this financial assessment.

Do I need to take out the entire amount I'm eligible for?

In order to maintain equity in the home the borrower can request an amount that is less than the one they are eligible for. If they decide to borrow a higher amount in the future this would require refinancing the loan with a new reverse mortgage, and would have to pay closing costs once again. Be aware that interest is paid only on the amount paid out, however closing costs could vary based on the size of loan limits.

What are the closing costs for a reverse mortgage ? And what do I do to pay them?

You could use a portion of the funds from the loan to pay the majority of the expenses of an HECM. If you choose this option it reduces the total amount of loan that is available to you by the exact amount. It is also possible to pay for them separately however, of course.

The HECM loan comes with a variety of costs and fees according to:

Mortgage Insurance Premium

The insurance is a year-long expense, and is priced at 1.25 percent of the current balance of the loan. This mortgage insurance assures you that you'll get the monthly installment due to you, regardless of the lender fails to pay.

It also offers protection to ensure that when the time arrives to sell the property and the proceeds of the sale don't cover the total amount due, you (or the estate of your) is not held accountable for the difference.

You could finance the mortgage insurance cost as part of the loan, but every time you decide not to pay for the costs at the time they are due, it decreases the amount available.

To find out the details about how Mortgage Insurance Premiums work, ask this query.

Origination Fee

A origination charge is among the fees you have to pay an institution to process an HECM loan. A HECM origination fee could be as high as $2500 if your home's worth is lower than $125,000. If your home's value is over $125,000, lenders may charge 2.2% of the initial $200,000 value of your home's worth plus 1percent of the value above $200,000. HECM origination fees are not allowed to exceed $6,000 at any time.

Servicing Fee

Lenders may charge fees to service your HECM loan throughout the period that it's in force. Servicing can include tasks such as sending your accounts statements as well as disbursing loan proceeds, and making sure that you're fully in compliance with conditions of the loan, including paying your real estate taxes as well as the cost of hazard insurance.

The lender is allowed the right to charge monthly service fee not exceeding $30 when the loan is secured by an interest that is adjusted once a year, and not more than $35 when the interest rate changes each month.

The lender may decide to include this fee as part of your mortgage rates (making an increase in order to cover the cost). The lender could also subtract the cost from your funds. If that is the case the monthly fee for servicing is added to the loan balance and the available funds are reduced.

Third Party Costs

Costs for closing from third parties may be a result of inspections, surveys recording costs, appraisal as well as title search and title insurance tax assessments, reports on credit, and other charges.

The only HECM charges that lenders do not control is the first mortgage insurance cost, along with the monthly fees. Costs vary a significant in between lenders therefore it is advisable to conduct some comparison shopping on charges and fees.

Consider how much each lender you're considering charge for the origination fee, all third party closing charges, the monthly servicing fee, and, most importantly, an interest charge. Some lenders may claim the interest rates they offer are based upon the specific rate index and an "margin." In the event that they say that, inquire about what the current interest rate is currently.

It is perfectly acceptable and, in addition, extremely smart to inform every lender that you're comparison shopping. In many cases, this can encourage them to reduce fees or, in certain cases, reduce certain fees entirely. They are more flexible than they would like to let you know.

Chapter 15: The Master Lease Option

If you are looking to make money through real estate and build an income-producing portfolio of properties that make you a successful investor for the long run This section is the most crucial part of this book. By using this strategy, in this Golden Age of real estate investing, you could make wealth that's greater than you've ever imagined or imagined for yourself. The method I'm talking about is called the Master Lease Option.

This technique may not be very well-known yet, but it's been in use for long periods of time. "Lease Option" is a term that "lease option" usually is used to describe single-family residential properties, however"master lease" is a more specific term "master lease" is typically used to describe commercial multi-family developments.

The ability to control an asset with the option of a master lease is the most effective way for a new real estate investor with no knowledge to acquire multifamily properties. The master lease option grants you total control over the property and then you have the option to sublease units and receive all rents.

There will be plenty of possibilities to purchase apartments with the option of a master lease in the Golden Age of real estate? Sure, there will be.

The advantages of using an option to master lease for buying real estate are many.

* You can purchase without putting any cash down

* You will be in complete control over the property, without appraisals, banks, or real estate agents

* Any net profit that is greater than the lease amount is a pure profit for you.

• Rapidly increase cash flow by reducing costs and growing the amount of revenue

* When equity is built up it is a breeze

* You'll have the choice to purchase the property at a predetermined price regardless of the worth in the house at time of time period that you have to pay for your master lease.

It's crucial to remember that the master lease as well as the purchase option constitute two separate agreements that should be written in separate agreements. If you make a purchase option, you'll only have the option to purchase the building, but not the obligation or requirement to purchase the building.

There's a chance that you'll come across a deal that's just too tempting for you to miss, however you're not sure whether you're able to turn it around. With a master lease option you can have the option of resigning in the event that things don't go as planned for you!

A purchase option contract provides you numerous advantages for buyers. If you're buying a depressed apartment, it offers the buyer the opportunity to improve the situation. If you aren't able to change the situation, you should not exercise your purchase option. If you're not very experienced with experience running an apartment building this gives you an chance to test whether you're capable of achieving success without spending a dime.

Utilizing a master lease option provides you with the chance to enhance the property to increase capital appreciation and also to fund it using the income generated by the property. Be sure to include the capital improvement clause into the agreement to ensure that you are able to accomplish this. Through capital improvements and improving the rate of vacancy it is possible to increase the value to your property. A lot of people undertake projects like this , and then find a buyer , and then make a cash payment before the term of the option expires.

A SOLUTION to the problem of banks

With a master lease option, you will be able to avoid the hassle and be able to do banking. If you have no prior experience dealing with apartments, banks most likely won't offer you the loan needed to purchase. They also are concerned about distressed properties which is a different issue that someone could face. If you can prove to an institution that you do not just have knowledge, but also an experience in turnaround, they'll be more open to working with them later on. You could even get financing for the first property you purchased following an effective turnaround.

This strategy can be employed to buy any kind of property, however the most effective and efficient use for this method is for apartment properties. There's already an established client base, and by signing the agreement, you'll be able to find ways to decrease expenses and boost profits to boost the net operating profit of your property.

If you sign an agreement for a master lease option it is essential to have an attorney assist you with the contract and also have your attorney write the agreement if the seller is in agreement. Let your real estate lawyer conduct a title search and investigate the property. It is important to know whether there are any liens that are attached to the house, and in case they are, you must determine the type of lien they are. It is also recommended to put money into an appraisal to ensure that you can get a current and accurate assessment for the home.

After all due diligence is completed with a valid agreement in place you'll need to visit the County Clerk's Office and record the master lease as well as buy option.

In my view, is the most effective way to invest in real estate in any kind of market. It is possible to find an opportunity to buy with this strategy before it is too late. Golden Age of real estate starts. This will require a lot of due diligence, however. I'd suggest waiting until the perfect time to do so and then committing this time for analyze and develop a strategy. The virtue of patience is.

USING THIS STRATEGY TO GET RICH

This strategy can be used to purchase mobile homes as well as hotels, office buildings as well as retail strip malls. I am convinced that this strategy is most effective with apartment-style buildings, but even though other kinds of properties are desirable but it is essential to consider that everyone will need an area to live in. This way of thinking about things has become more attractive for me as I get more proficient in my own property-related career.

The purchase of apartment buildings using Master Lease Option is the most efficient method to make money I've heard of. If you take on one task at a time, reversing the project around, and then handing off day-to-day tasks to a reliable managing the property, you will be able to build up a property portfolio in just five years, which will prepare you for the future and make everyone jealous. The most exciting part is that the greatest five-year win we'll ever experience in our lifetimes lies just in front of us!

The purchase of an apartment with the master lease option is not a fantasy sky idea. It's very feasible and is very popular. I recently purchased the property I first bought commercially in this manner and I doubt that I'd consider purchasing an additional property using "conventional techniques". In 2017-2022, you'll find many more sellers who are willing to sell their homes using this method than they have ever been. In the coming years, vacancies and evictions will increase, which will increase the enthusiasm of sellers. There is plenty of potential to build equity in the home in the years to come after you buy it.

Although this is the most efficient option to purchase an apartment for many people, it's probably not the only option to go about it. Many of us don't have the 30percent down payment or the financial requirements that go with lending guidelines for commercial properties. In addition, those who are qualified and have sufficient funds to fund an initial down payment will not be able to get financing. The master lease can be your best friend and most sellers will be open to it.

The most effective way to enter in to the master lease without a deposit is to arrange the deal to ensure that the master lease payment are equal to the current NOI (also known as the net operating revenue). This means you're essentially agreeing to manage the property on a free basis. This is how you'll explain to the owner however, your primary goal is to grow the operating profit as fast as you can.

In the event that the landlord has maintained rents lower than market rates The quickest and simplest method to increase the NOI is to increase rents. It is possible to do this all at once or after leases run out and renewed. Filling vacant spaces is the most effective method to increase your NOI. In the kind of climate that which the Golden Age will bring, there are many homes which are only 65 to 70 percent filled. If you can fill these vacant spaces, you'll be on a speedy path to rapid profit. Not just in terms of your monthly cash flow as well as in relation to the equity positions.

If you are looking to purchase an apartment or multi-family home that has a master lease option and master lease option, you shouldn't be worried about how credit-worthy you are. I wasn't required to provide my credit history when purchasing my house using this method. I've made sure to inquire about those who purchased using this method and have reported back the similar things. If you're sensitive to your credit score, do not expect to be asked to furnish a credit history. If this happens, it's only a blip and you should be sure that the next property owner isn't going to ask.

There may be a time in which a seller doesn't wish to do anything with the property, but wants to keep the title. If you encounter the situation, cut 20% off what you planned to offer, and odds are that the seller will agree. It is possible to advertise your interest in property in such situations online or by printing flyers and bringing them to the real estate investing group gatherings.

Based on the knowledge you've gathered from this guide, you've got the necessary knowledge to be an owner of a building without making any investment of your own money and without putting your credit at risk. What you need to do is to act, and you'll be able to see the results.

The time we are in will give us the chance of the lifetime to make it rich. The Great Depression, more millionaires were made than at any other time during the entire history of this country. United States. The current Golden Age will be no any different. I wish you all the best of luck when you create your fortune.

Conclusion

Flipping houses or investing in houses can be a very lucrative business when you approach it the right manner. At present, I have sixteen rental units out. What happens when the portfolio grows is that I'm in a position to pay off loans on a couple of them, so that I own them completely. In the meantime, I earn more. If I require money fast, I have the option of getting an loan based on the property's worth, or dispose of an investment in order to fund my next venture. The decision is my however it can take a while to reach the point when you have the option of. While you're at it you have to keep lenders satisfied and ensure that mortgage payments are always paid in time.

When you earn a name as a provider of top-quality houses, you can expand your options and follow the same model like Property Brothers. Property Brothers do where a couple buys a home however, you offer them an average price to help them bring the house to the level they desire. I've done it several times, it can be an effective venture in times when cash isn't in plentiful supply , but you need to be on the job. People will be willing to pay for a properly designed package, and you must to establish your name so that more people come to know about the products that you offer and be willing to give you their hard-earned money. If you choose to go this direction, make sure to purchase software that allows you to present prospective buyers with the possibilities you have with the house they purchase.

Investment in property is a fantastic option to put money into your future.

Once the mortgages are paid, you own the bricks and mortar however, be sure to keep the property in good condition and when you look over prospective properties, be sure that there aren't any issues with the structure that could create problems for maintenance. It is important to make sure that your investment is secure and purchasing something that isn't fully aware of repair requirements is a risky proposition at best.

If you maintain your work up to a standard and use professionals you can believe will not take shortcuts, you will earn an excellent reputation, but you can also provide your investment properties secure future source of income as you be aware of the condition of these properties. You'll be aware of any repairs required in the term of any tenancy, and deal promptly time. When you do this you're protecting your future income, therefore do not think of it as something negative to consider. It's an integral part of owning a home and allows you get the most out of the investment you make in a house.

Befriend the local planning department as they may have to assist you in the event that you want to make any structural changes on the outside of your home, which naturally require planning approval. It is important to keep up-to-date with changes to the law in regards to codes , and ensure that your contractors remain up to date to ensure that the houses you're building provide security for tenants or people who are willing to buy the houses which you offer available for purchase. Cuts and tricks never work. They always come back. Fittings and fixtures that are of low quality do not have the same longevity as high-end ones. It is possible to use different types of flooring to lower your costs however, while you keep your budget running, you might need to alter the finishes in order to stay within your budget. Knowing your vendors and the items they have on hand, you could just need to alter the quality of your countertop to help you save the cost of having to install the best pipes for a bathroom that wasn't up to the latest standards, yet wasn't accounted for in the initial quotes. It's all about maintaining a balance in everything and, most importantly, making sure that your home is secure refuges for families that purchase them or rent them.

For a final reminder, curb appeal is the most important factor. If your home is done and ready for the open day Make sure it is appealing to those looking from the outside of your home. The landscaping and the way you present your home with a welcoming appearance will add a lot of value in the chance of selling. People are drawn to homes they feel proud of, not an unattractive house laid out on a poor plot. It's the impression the house creates that can make an impact on the outcome.

www.ingramcontent.com/pod-product-compliance
Lightning Source LLC
Chambersburg PA
CBHW071222210326
41597CB00016B/1906